Visual Manna's Teaching American History Through Art

II Chronicles 7:14

If my people, which are called by my name, shall humble themselves, and pray, and seek my face, and turn from their wicked ways; then will I hear from heaven, and will forgive their sin, and will heal their land.

by
Sharon Jeffus
Illustrated by Richard Jeffus

Copyright 1997
Visual Manna
P.O. Box 553
Salem, Missouri 65560

ISBN 0-9677386-4-4

We would like to thank the Boston Museum of Fine Arts for their permission to use the images *George Washington* by Gilbert Stuart, *Thunderstorm at Sea* by Washington Alston and *Paul Revere* by Copely seen in this book. We also want to credit the Dover Pictorial Archives and the Borderline Collection of Clip Art for some of the pictures seen here.

Table of Contents

These lessons are supplements to a study of American history. They are multi-level and are appropriate for grades one through ten. Use this Table of Contents to supplement other teaching texts. There are several publishing companies that carry wonderful books about American history. A History of US--The New Nation by Joy Hakim carried by Common Sense Press is an excellent text to compliment this book. Diana Waring--History Alive Publications has excellent materials for studying history. Greenleaf Publications also carries an array of American history materials that work well. Bob Jones University and Abeka carry primary texts that complement this study. Use this book for delightful activities for visual and kinesthetic learners!

Introduction 3	The Cattle Drive. 32
Gilbert Stuart—George Washington 7	Pioneer Dolls 33
The Boston Massacre. 8	Rebus 35
American Symbols. 9	Pictographs. 36
Cigar Store Indians 11	The Avalanche 37
John Singleton Copely 12	Paper Quilling 38
Paul Revere's Ride. 13	The End of the Civil War. 39
Quill Pens. 14	One Point Perspective 40
Declaration of Independence 15	The Beginning of Cities. 45
Quilting in America 16	Thomas Nast—Editorial Cartoons. 46
Early Pioneers 17	George Washington Carver 49
American Seascapes. 18	The Teddy Bear 50
Johnny Appleseed 19	Purple Mountain Majesty. 52
Apples 20	Old Fashioned Christmas. 53
California Maps and Trails. 21	Currier and Ives 54
The Threat of Indians 22	Mount Rushmore 55
Portrait of Sitting Bull 23	Calendars 57
Drawing the Face in Perspective 24	Tiffany Glass 58
The Buffalo in American History. 25	Pottery 59
Americans Braving the Storms 26	American Indians. 60
Sandpainting 27	N.Y. City—Center of Art? 61
Robert Fulton Artist & Scientist 29	Merging Science and Art 62
Sheep vs. Cattle 30	Remington & the Setting Sun 64
Sheep 31	Timeline Test 65

Introduction

In introducing this book on <u>American History Through Art</u>, I want to say that this subject is vast and comprehensive. One book would not be adequate to cover the topic in detail. I will begin by mentioning several artists that you will want to study as you are studying periods of American History. I have several mentioned in the following pages with corresponding lessons, but I want to mention some that you can research yourself if you choose too. The following pictures with corresponding lessons can be found in <u>Visual Manna Complete Art Curriculum</u>. You can also look these artists up in reference books or an encyclopedia. Edward Hicks is a wonderful American artist whose picture *The Peaceable Kingdom* shows a peaceful meeting between the settlers and the Indians. *Fur Traders on the Missouri* by George Caleb Bingham shows us life on the Missouri and Mississippi Rivers in the mid 1800's. Albert Bierdstadt's *The Rocky Mountains* show us what the west was like at the time of Lewis and Clark. *The Robie House* by Frank Lloyd Wright shows us America's greatest architect. *Portrait of the Artist's Mother* by Whistler, *The Torn Hat* by Thomas Sully, and *The Banjo Lesson* by Tanner are all wonderful American portraits. We also see *The Bronco Buster* by the great western artist Remington. In Visual Manna II, we see *The Little Spaniard* by George Catlin, a great artist who concentrated on showing the lifestyle and wonder of the American Indian. We also have *Breezing Up* by Winslow Homer, the great American seascape artist. Visual Manna I also has a lesson called "Pottery" that would make a good study because of the Indian pottery that is so much a part of our heritage. Visual Manna sells Indian pottery clay and also authentic Indian face paint in our catalog that you might want to incorporate in your study. Look up the following addresses on the internet to find these various artists:

Audubon
http://www.audubon.org/nas/art.html
Up the Missouri With Audubon
http://www.usd.edu/"jwortham/magpie/harris.html
Charles Russell
http://www.maturityusa.com/travel/russell.html
Remington
http://www.northnet.org/broncho/
Catlin
http://www.usd.edu/~jwortham/crow/catlin.html

Norman Rockwell is a very well known period illustrator who portrayed the idyllic small town America in the early 1900's. Currier and Ives were a lithography firm that published many 19th century prints showing the manner, people, and general personality of the time. Enjoy studying all these marvelous American artists!

America! She has inspired melodies that stir our hearts -

> "From the oceans, to the prairies, to the mountains white with snow..."
> "O'er the land of the free and the home of the brave..."
> "This land is your land, this land is my land..."
> "Sweet land of liberty, of Thee I sing..."

America! She has produced poetry that touches the soul -

> "Listen, my children, and you shall hear
> Of the midnight ride of Paul Revere..."
> "...Give me your tired, your poor,
> Your huddled masses yearning to breathe free,
> The wretched refuse of your teeming shore.
> Send these, the homeless, tempest-tost to me,
> I lift my lamp beside the golden door!"
> "Behind him lay the gray Azores,
> Behind the Gates of Hercules;
> Before him not the ghost of shores,
> Before him only shoreless seas.
> The good mate said: "Now must we pray,
> For lo! the very stars are gone.
> Brave Admiral, speak; what shall I say?"
> "Why, say, 'Sail on! sail on! and on!'"

America! She has yielded a harvest of speeches that quicken our spirits -

> "I know not what course others may take; but as for me, give me liberty, or give me death!"
> "I only regret that I have but one life to lose for my country."
> "Fourscore and seven years ago our fathers brought forth upon this continent a new nation, coceived in liberty, and dedicated to the proposition that all men are created equal..."

America! The music, the literature, the art of America express the unique and precious heritage of our country. Let us not be content to merely know:

> the names - Columbus, Washington, Lincoln;
> the dates - 1492, 1776, 1861;
> the places - Plymouth Rock, Boston Harbor, Gettysburg; but let us strive to comprehend the reasons behind them. Let us learn the why's and the wherefore's, the heart and soul of our nation, the creative expression which will transport us from a dull knowing to a rich comprehension.

America! Our home, our responsibility, our legacy.

> "Let us raise a standard to which the wise and honest can repair;
>   the rest is in the hands of God." George Washington

by Diana Waring (History Alive Publications)
For a wonderful learning adventure contact History Alive, 122 W. Grant, Spearfish, SD, 57783. They carry materials that combine music, history and hands on fun in a unique way! Contact them for a catalog.

How to Use a Grid

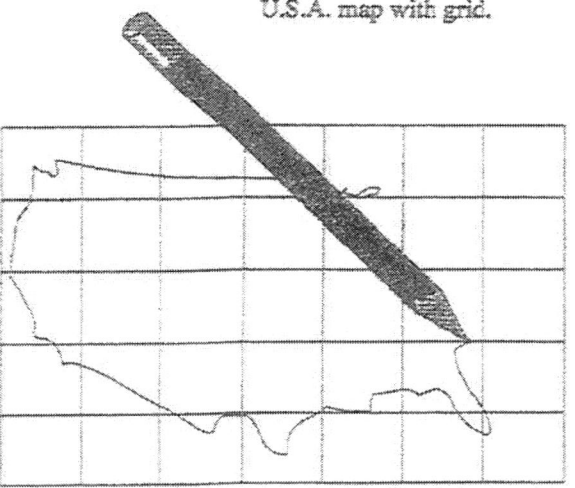

U.S.A. map with grid.

Outline of map being reproduced by carefully drawing line over same grid points.

In this book there are many opportunities to do drawings using the grid. This is an optional way to copy a master work of art. Many artists in the past and artists today use a grid in their work. Copying great works of art is one way to learn technique and grow as an artist. Following are directions for using a grid. There are two ways to use a grid. One way is to do the entire outline first, and then go back and complete the inside. The other way is to do one single square at a time, completing each one before going on to the next. Whichever way you use, try to remember to draw what you see, and not what you think you see. Doing a grid can help you become a better artist by letting you see the relationship between each separate part of a whole drawing. Remember that using a grid is only one way of several in which an artist uses to copy a picture.

George Washington, 1796, Stuart, Gilbert, U.S., 1755-1828, Oil on canvas, 47 3/4 x 37 in. (121.3 x 94.0 cm) CREDIT LINE: William Francis Warden Fund, John H. and Erestine A. Payne Fund, Commonwealth Cultural Preservation Trust. Jointly owned by the Museum of Fine Arts, Boston and the National Portrait Gallery, Washington, D.C. Courtesy: Museum of Fine Arts, Boston

George Washington

Gilbert Stuart--The Great Portrait Artist

We can thank Gilbert Stuart for giving us wonderful portraits of our founding fathers. There were no cameras, and he had that special gift of capturing the spirit of a person on canvas. Some artists can do pictures of people, but they seem to miss that certain something that brings the canvas to life and really captures the essence of a person, but Gilbert Stuart has over 1000 portraits to his credit and each is a masterpiece portrait. He painted George Washington, Thomas Jefferson, Benjamin Franklin, and James Madison, just to name a few. Did he have to work and study to achieve this high degree of technical expertise? He was born in Rhode Island, but went to England in 1775 to study under the master artist Benjamin West. In England, he was greatly influenced by Thomas Gainsborough and Joshua Reynolds. Here is one of his well know portraits. Use the grid to draw your own

picture of George Washington. Now try to draw him freehand, just using your sight to get the proportion correct. Which way do you prefer?

The Boston Massacre

Some artists capture moments in history. This picture is of a famous moment in the Revolutionary War. *The Boston Massacre* was done by Paul Revere, an artist, a silversmith, and a great patriot of the revolution. This is a rendering of the original. When you are studying great battles in our nation's history, it is interesting to also look at art done at that particular time about the great events. Notice the repeated design shown by the soldiers. A visual rhythm is created. Overlapping is done by placing one soldier in front of the other. The soldiers in the front are larger than the soldiers in the back. The buildings in the background are perfect examples of one point perspective. See the lesson on one point perspective after "The Civil War" lesson and try to make a room in your house. Can you do a picture of a recent news event?

American Symbols -- The Rattlesnake and the Eagle

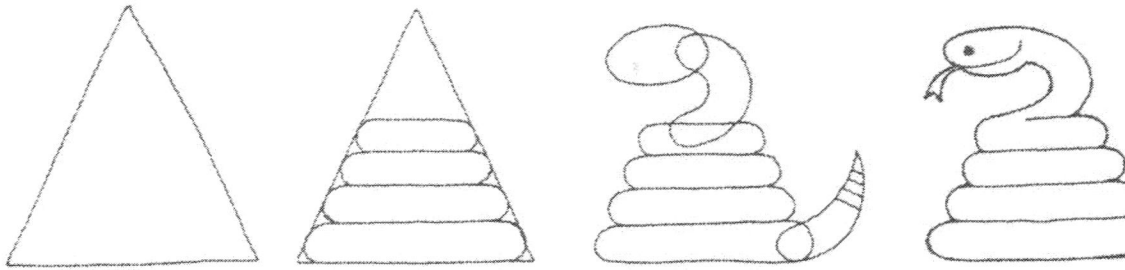

Did you know that Benjamin Franklin actually suggested that the rattlesnake would make a good American symbol? It was native to America. Did it have qualities that were like America? When the rattlesnake is left alone, it is peaceful and calm, but when you step on it, it is deadly...just like America. The snake gives a warning before it strikes, hardly ever loses, and never surrenders. During the Revolutionary War days, the rattlesnake appeared on American flags with mottos like "Don't tread on me!" and "Liberty or Death." Look at the pictures of some of these revolutionary flags. Use an old blind stick (these work well, as they are not sharp, but will hold a paper flag) and a piece of 12" by 18" white paper. Use a glue gun or white craft glue to glue the paper on the blind or stick. Design a flag that would make anyone think twice before going to war with America.

The Eagle

The American bald eagle was the final selection for the symbol of America, competing with the wild turkey, the rattlesnake, and the goose. The eagle is symbolic of majesty and strength. The Indians knew the eagle as the "thunderbird" whose wings caused

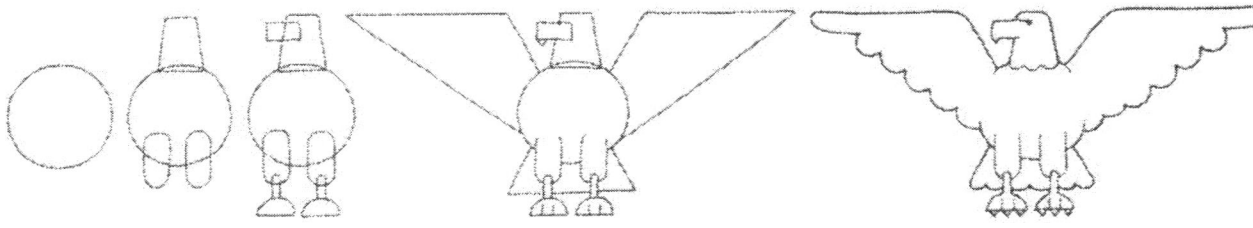

thunder. Follow the directions for drawing the eagle using the grid. Can you hide a message about American in his wings? Use the grid and draw the eagle on this page.

There are two ways to use a grid. One way is to just do one single square at a time, completing each one before going on to the next. The other way is to do the entire outline, and then go back and complete the inside. Whichever way you try, remember to draw what you see and not what you think you see. Doing a grid can help you become a better artist, by letting you see the relationship between each separate part of a whole drawing.

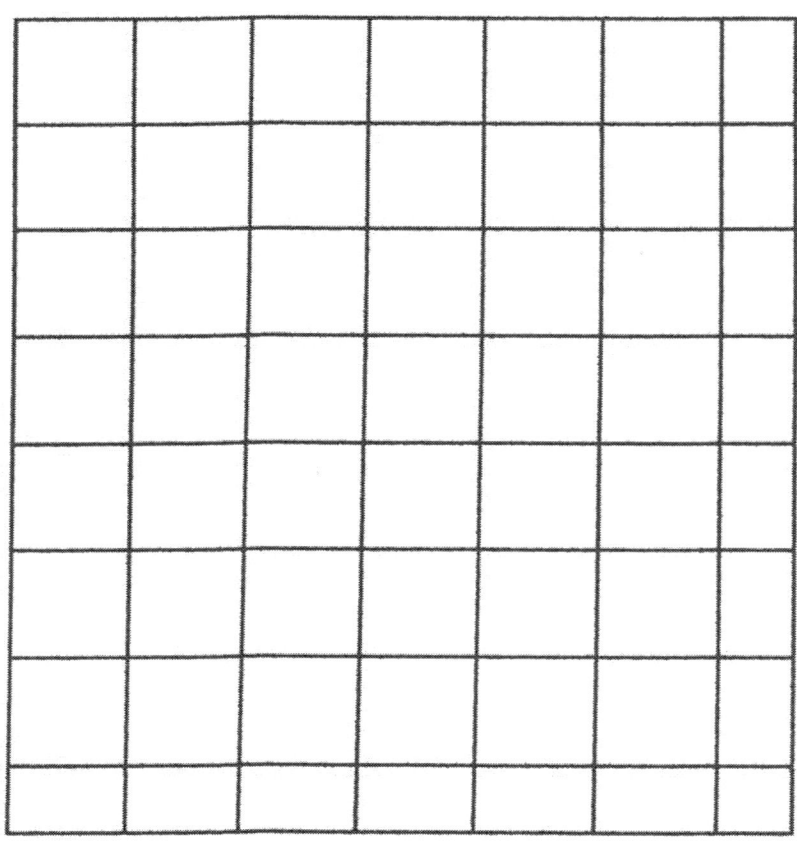

Cigar Store Figures

Can you even imagine that this was a wonderful art form in our American past? From our colonial past to the beginning of the 20th century, carved large wooden figures graced the entrance of many American stores of all kinds. Just as in the Middle Ages when heraldry was used for the illiterate people to recognize what something was, wooden figures were used to identify what the store was all about. One of the outstanding examples that we have of American folk sculpture is the Cigar Store Indian. When steam ships replaced sailing vessels, many unemployed ship figurehead carvers went to work carving cigar store figures. Many characters of history are shown using tobacco in some form. Is this similar to the many billboards we see today advertising tobacco products? Get a piece of wood or soap and just try to carve a figure. This would be subtractive sculpture because once you take it off, you cannot glue or put it back on like you could with clay. Another great idea is to make some sawdust clay (8 cups of sawdust, one cup of wheat paste, one half cup of salt), mix and add water. Now sculpture something, (this is additive sculpture) and then when it dries you can sand it and paint it.

John Singleton Copely

Copely was probably the most popular artist in American colonial society. He did wonderful portraits. This is just one example of his work. Notice that he puts Paul Revere's profession into the picture. Because he was a silversmith, Copely puts that in his portrait. Make a portrait of a person in history and use surroundings and objects to tell something about the person.

Paul Rever, 1768, Copley, John Singleton, U.S., 1738-1815, Oil on canvas, 35 1/8 x 28 1/2 in. (89.2 x 72.4 cm)
CREDIT LINE: Gift of Joseph W. Rever, William B. Rever, and Edward H. R. Rever, Courtesy, Museum of Fine Arts, Boston

Paul Revere's Ride

This picture is *Paul Revere's Ride* by Reid. What are some of the things the artist does to make the picture look realistic? Notice that the things in the foreground are larger than things in the background. Notice the shade difference between the front of the house and the side of the house in the background. Diagonal lines show movement. Notice the diagonal lines in the horse and rider. This picture is also a one point perspective. The artist has framed the picture with the classical Greek Ionic Columns. If you have the <u>Book of Virtues</u> by William Bennett or a similar text, read "The Midnight Ride of Paul Revere," by Henry Wadsworth Longfellow. Can you do a picture of this event and paint it with brushes and create the same feeling the poet has created with words?

Quill Pens -- Painting on Feathers

In early America, school children used pens made from small carved twigs or feathers. A wood nib pen was just a carved twig.

Have you ever found a feather on the ground? You know feathers are lost a few at a time from both sides of the body so the bird is still balanced evenly. There are two kinds of feathers; contour and down. Contour feathers are found on the wings, tail and body of the bird. The strands, or barbs, of the feather lock together. Down feathers are the fluffy feathers used for warmth. This art project only involves contour feathers. I went to an art show recently and found a lady who did beautiful paintings on feathers. She used acrylic paint and small brushes. Why not paint a feather? If you cut the tip of the feather at an angle, you will have a feather quill pen.

Strain the berries and throw the pulp away. Add the salt and vinegar and stir. Can you imagine a group of men signing a very important document using a feather?

Recipe for berry ink:
1/2 cup ripe berries
1/2 teaspoon salt
1/2 teaspoon vinegar

IN CONGRESS, July 4, 1776.

The unanimous Declaration of the thirteen united States of America,

When in the Course of human events, it becomes necessary for one people to dissolve the political bands which have connected them with another, and to assume among the powers of the earth, the separate and equal station to which the Laws of Nature and of Nature's God entitle them, a decent respect to the opinions of mankind requires that they should declare the causes which impel them to the separation.

We hold these truths to be self-evident, that all men are created equal, that they are endowed by their Creator with certain unalienable Rights, that among these are Life, Liberty and the pursuit of Happiness.—That to secure these rights, Governments are instituted among Men, deriving their just powers from the consent of the governed,—That whenever any Form of Government becomes destructive of these ends, it is the Right of the People to alter or to abolish it, and to institute new Government, laying its foundation on such principles and organizing its powers in such form, as to them shall seem most likely to effect their Safety and Happiness. Prudence, indeed, will dictate that Governments long established should not be changed for light and transient causes; and accordingly all experience hath shewn, that mankind are more disposed to suffer, while evils are sufferable, than to right themselves by abolishing the forms to which they are accustomed. But when a long train of abuses and usurpations, pursuing invariably the same Object evinces a design to reduce them under absolute Despotism, it is their right, it is their duty, to throw off such Government, and to provide new Guards for their future security.—Such has been the patient sufferance of these Colonies; and such is now the necessity which constrains them to alter their former Systems of Government. The history of the present King of Great Britain is a history of repeated injuries and usurpations, all having in direct object the establishment of an absolute Tyranny over these States. To prove this, let Facts be submitted to a candid world.

He has refused his Assent to Laws, the most wholesome and necessary for the public good.

He has forbidden his Governors to pass Laws of immediate and pressing importance, unless suspended in their operation till his Assent should be obtained; and when so suspended, he has utterly neglected to attend to them.

He has refused to pass other Laws for the accommodation of large districts of people, unless those people would relinquish the right of Representation in the Legislature, a right inestimable to them and formidable to tyrants only.

He has called together legislative bodies at places unusual, uncomfortable, and distant from the depository of their Public Records, for the sole purpose of fatiguing them into compliance with his measures.

He has dissolved Representative Houses repeatedly, for opposing with manly firmness his invasions on the rights of the people.

He has refused for a long time, after such dissolutions, to cause others to be elected; whereby the Legislative powers, incapable of Annihilation, have returned to the People at large for their exercise; the State remaining in the mean time exposed to all the dangers of invasion from without, and convulsions within.

This is a copy of the original writing of the Constitution of the United States. Notice the beautiful handwriting that is seen in the document. At the time of the writing of this document, beautiful handwriting was something to be proud of. During the 1800's, collecting autographs of friends was a favorite thing to do.

First, copy the first line of this document exactly---as close as you can---to the original document. Now create your own document or special letter, using the best handwriting you can.

If someone asks you to sign their yearbook, what clever statement can you write?

Quilting in America

In the Revolutionary War times, the English taxes on clothing became so high that Americans began wearing their own homemade clothing again. Before that time, many Americans went to clothing shops and bought garments imported from England. A renewed interest in home sewing occurred and ladies sewing bees became a new popular activity. This grew into making the wonderful quilts that are so richly a part of our heritage. Here is a project for making a quilt like design. Here also is an exciting project for children to experiment with different mediums of paint. Fill a muffin tin with 3 colors of liquid food coloring, three colors of tempera paint, three colors of water color paint and three colors colored chalk. Use these different mediums to create a patchwork quilt. Do six squares of equal size (you can fold a piece of 11 1/2 by 18 white paper) and experiment with the different mediums. Use a black permanent marker to outline and emphasize certain shapes. You will have a finished design that will have variety in design and use of medium. If you put these together in one shape, a quilt design will occur. You can also use wallpaper books that have been discontinued and cut them out into quilt designs.

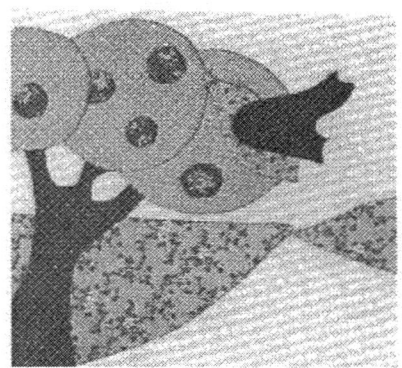

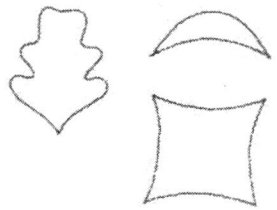

Early Pioneers Dying Clothing

Can you imagine how the early pioneers colored their clothing? Did you know you can easily create natural dyes that are a lot like the dyes the Indians and pioneers used? Look for the following plants that are available in your area.

onion -- makes a yellow color
goldenrod -- makes a beige/yellow color
blue lupine -- makes a pale green color
oak bark -- makes a dark brown color
wild holly berries -- makes a pale pink color
blueberries -- makes a blue color
poke weed -- makes a purple-black color (There are handwritten notes from the Civil War written with ink berry that are still legible).
blackberries -- makes a purple color
walnuts -- make a greenish yellow color (chartreuse).

Slowly bring the mixture of plants and water (8 cups of water) to a boil for one hour. Wet the fabric you will dye with water and then add it to the pot for at least one hour. If you want a patterned effect, use rubber bands and wrap them tightly around the material. Hang the finished dyed cloth outside to dry. You have now accomplished something that your early ancestors probably did on a regular basis to make their clothing more attractive!

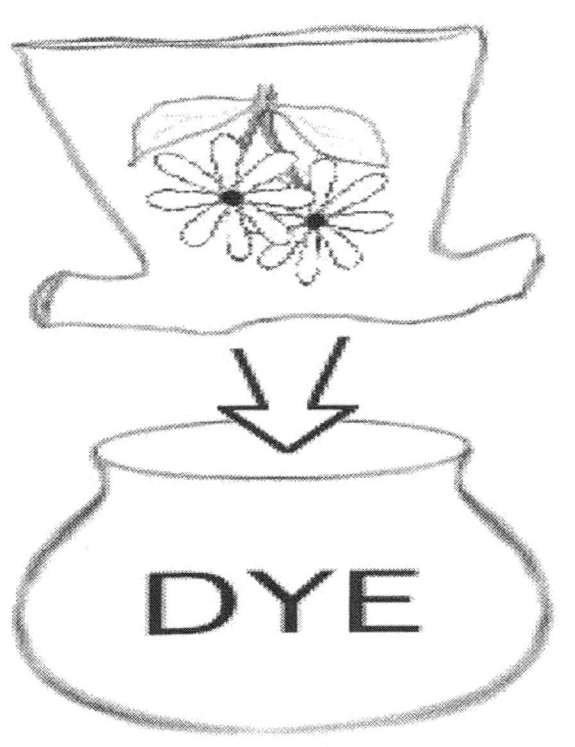

American Seascapes

Look at this powerful seascape by Washington Allston. He was an American artist who painted in the 1800's. Notice the diagonal lines in the picture. Diagonal lines show movement. You can see a ship in the background and one in the foreground. Although the ship in the background is a very large ship, it looks small in the distance. Things in the foreground look larger and things in the background look smaller. An excellent project for a child in art is to do a study on waves and then do a torn paper picture of the waves in the ocean. They can color a sheet of paper several colors of blue and then tear in wavy long strips to make an interesting picture of waves, or they can use various shades of blue construction or tissue paper. When they have finished layering the torn paper, it will look like waves. This should be glued on a piece of heavy paper or poster board. Now they can use their scissors and make a boat for their ocean. If they put the boat in the foreground of the picture, it will be very large. If they put it on the horizon line (the place where the ocean and sky meet), it will be much smaller. Ships were a very important part of America's history in the 1800's.

Johnny Appleseed

What would a study of America be without the wonderful story of Johnny Appleseed? Johnny Appleseed's real name was John Chapman. He was born in Massachusettes when the state was still part of the frontier. Johnny grew up to be very knowledgeable about herbs and plants, but particularly apples. He collected seeds from presses that made cider, so he could sell the seeds. He soon began giving the seeds away to settlers and pioneers heading west. When he was a young man, he headed to the state of Ohio where he walked leading a packhorse loaded down with apples. He would travel from settlement to settlement, planting apple trees. For almost 50 years he traveled through midwestern America. Here is a description of Johnny Appleseed. Can you draw a picture of him just from this description? He wore a long-handled pot on his head. He wore a coffee sack for a shirt (he cut holes in it for his arms). His pants were worn and ragged, and his feet were bare. Here is an excellent project for younger children. Look at pictures of the tree on a piece of poster board, mat board, or heavy cardboard. I suggest using poster paint or markers for the coloring. Now pop some popcorn and let them glue this

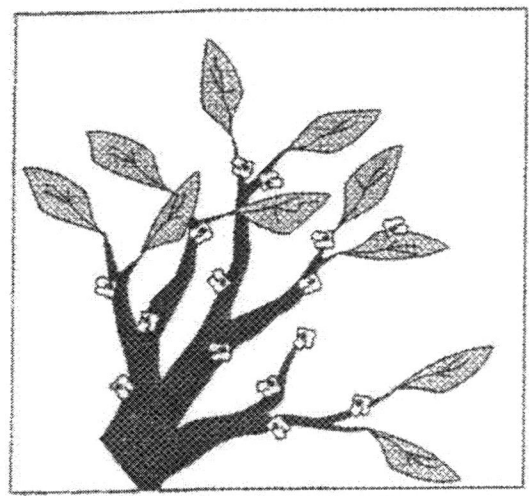

apple tree in blossom. Now have children draw the limbs of a tree and the leaves of a on the branches for flowers. Drawing an apple is also a good exercise for older children. Some very well known works of art contain apples and are called still life. Set up a still life of a bowl of apples. Be sure things are place in an uneven composition to add interest. Now allow them to sketch it out in pencil first and then paint it. There is a precious song about Johnny Appleseed. "Oh, the Lord is good to me, and so I thank the Lord---for giving me the things I need---the sun and the rain---and the apple seed---the Lord is good to me."

Apples

Americans love apples. Apples are flowering seed plants in the vascular plant family. In the days of early America, apple trees were grown from seed and date back to Massachusetts right after the Pilgrims arrived. Today apple trees are grown by grafting a bud or twig of an established apple tree onto a seedling tree. Some doctors suggest that an apple may help relieve flu and colds and a few dentists say that apples brush your teeth as good as a toothbrush. Drawing an apple is a simple task. Practice drawing an apple first and then a grouping of apples.

Draw some apples in a basket.

California Maps And Trails

This is a picture that appeared in the *Illustrated London News* from the writings of Fremont on the "Report of the Exploring Expeditions of 1842 and 43-44." It was required reading for immigrants. Fremont and his men were capable of surviving indefinitely because they were experienced explorers, but families that struck out for the west often encountered heartships and tragedy. A great idea for children is to make up an adventure board game (if you have access to the computer game "The Oregon Trail," this might inspire children with ideas). Here are some other map project ideas:

MAKING MAPS ACROSS THE CURRICULUM

1. TALK ABOUT MAPS AND THEIR IMPORTANCE. STUDY MAPS OF MODERN DAY AMERICA. HAVE EXAMPLES OF OLD MAPS OF AMERICA AVAILABLE IF POSSIBLE. IDEA FOR PROBLEM SOLVING -- WHILE STUDYING A PARTICULAR PLACE, OR A ROUTE SUCH AS THE NORTHWEST PASSAGE, OR THE ROUTE OF LEWIS AND CLARK---THE PROBLEM IS TO MAKE AN AUTHENTIC LOOKING 150 YEAR OLD MAP. ALLOW CHILDREN TO DOCUMENT THE PROCESS THAT THEY USED TO ACHIEVE AN AGED LOOK. SOME SUGGESTIONS MIGHT INCLUDE DRAWING THE MAP FIRST, AND THEN WRINKLING IT, AND SOAKING IT IN TEA AND SOAP. ETC.

2. USE MAT BOARD SCRAPS AND MODELING CLAY AND LEARN TOPOGRAPHY BY PUTTING MOUNTAINS, ETC. ON MAP.

3. MAKE A RECIPE FOR COOKIES AND USE MEASURING SKILLS AND THEN BAKE THE COOKIES ON A LARGE COOKIE PAN INTO ONE GIGANTIC COOKIE. USE RECIPE FOR EDIBLE CLAY AND MAKE TOPOGRAPHY. FINISH DETAILING WITH ICING.

4. READ ABOUT A CERTAIN SETTING IN GIANTS IN THE EARTH OR SARAH, PLAIN AND TALL. NOW ALLOW STUDENTS TO DRAW A MAP AFTER HEARING YOUR DESCRIPTION OF THE LAND. NOTICE THE VARIETY OF MAPS THAT ARE CREATED.

5. FIND OLD MAPS AND FREE MAPS AND MAKE FOLDERS AND BOOK COVERS FROM THESE TREASURES.

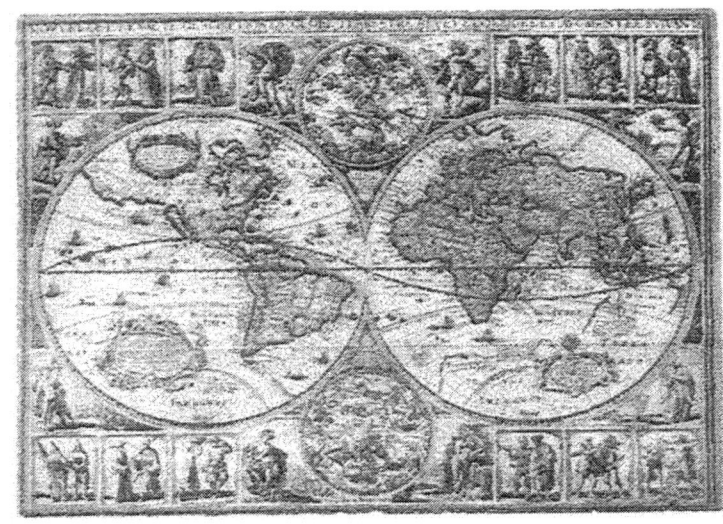

The Threat of Indians

Art is obviously a very powerful tool in swaying opinion. There were several well known works of art that came out showing Indians taking advantage of white women, and doing violent acts of savage killing. *The Murder of Jane McCrea* by John Vanderlyn, *The Abduction of Daniel Boone's Daughter by the Indians* by Carl Wimar, and *Osage Scalp Dance* by John Stanley are just some examples. This drawing of Indians gambling for the girl in the picture was published in *Harper's Weekly,* March 26, 1870. Just think of all the people in the east who were affected by this picture. In reality, cholera was a bigger threat than Indians on the wagon train trips out west.

Portrait of Sitting Bull

The dominant Indian figure in the last part of the Indian Wars of the northern plains was Sitting Bull. The picture of him was published in the *Illustrated London News* just before he got killed at wounded Knee. Use the grid on this page and draw the great Indian Chief Sitting Bull. Now draw a portrait of him using the guidelines on the following page. Which method did you prefer?

DRAWING THE FACE IN PROPORTION

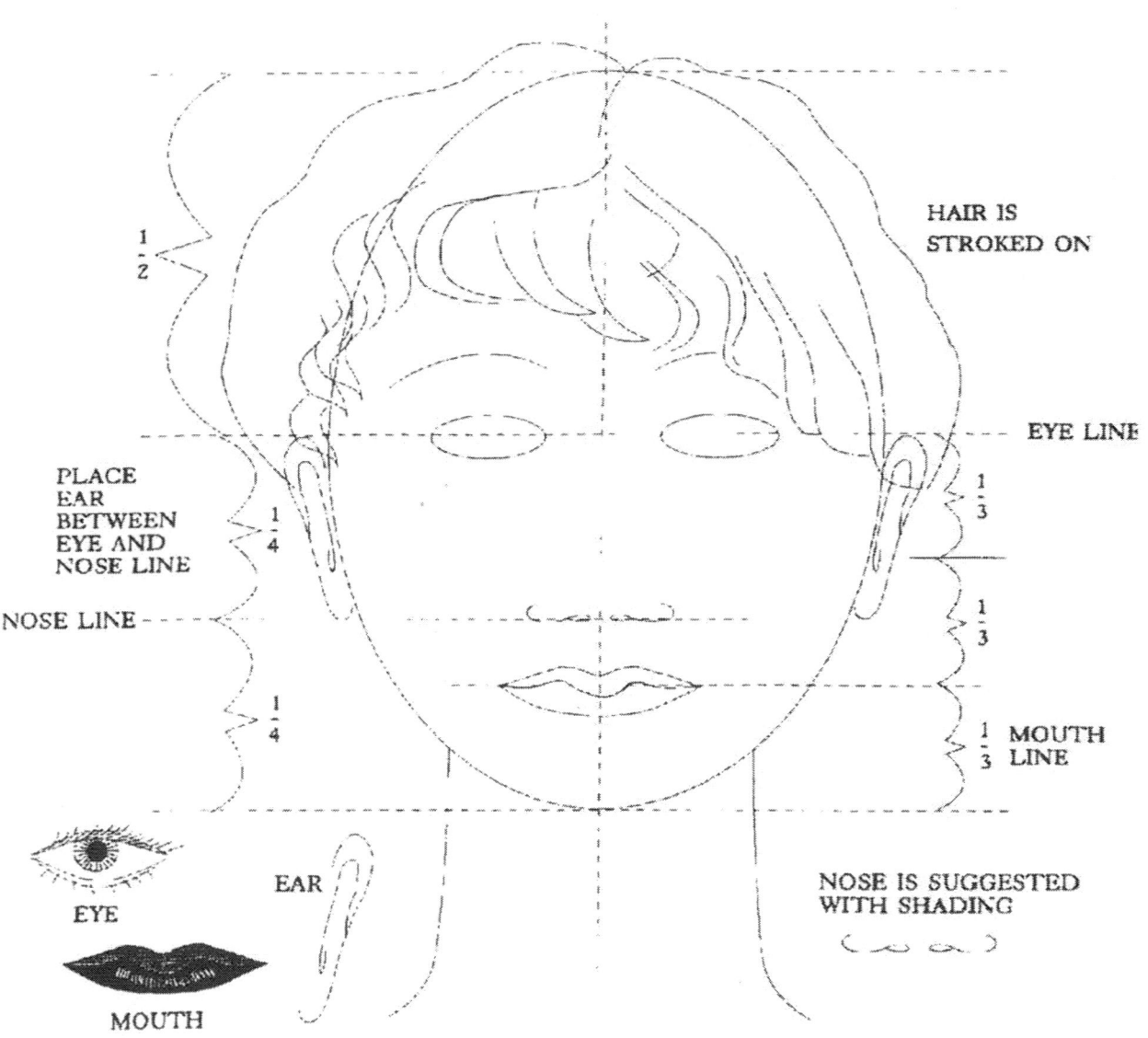

The Buffalo in American History

Here is a picture seen frequently in early American history---buffalo surrounding a train. One hundred years ago, buffalo roamed the American plains in huge numbers. Indian tribes used the hide, the meat, and even the bones. They made tepee covers, ropes, clothing, moccasins, etc. Some Indian tribes followed the buffalo herds. Before the 1860's there were estimated over seventy five million buffalo. When the railroad constructed tracks across the plains, professional hunters were instructed to kill the animals for meat. Buffalo Bill Cody supposedly got his name by killing over 4,280 buffalo in a year. People in the east came west to shoot the buffalo for fun. By 1900, buffalo had nearly become extinct. In 1913, the American Mint honored the buffalo with a coin called the Buffalo Nickel. Follow the directions on drawing a buffalo and design your own coin honoring this native American animal.

Americans Braving the Storms

Below is a picture that was published in *Harper's Weekly* in January of 1888. These are calvary soldiers, but many pioneers and settlers in the days of the early American west in winter went through severe blizzards like this. Allow children to do a picture of a scene from early America. Now students will make a snow scene with a different twist. A landscape is primarily a picture of natural scenery seen by the eye in one view. The place where the land and sky meet is the horizon line. If some of you live in a city, you might want to do a picture of your surroundings covered with snow. If it doesn't snow where you live, you can find a snow picture or use your imagination. Do your picture on white paper and use the brightest colors possible for the land and trees or houses. Leave much of the ground white. When you are finished with the scene, water down some white craft glue, paint the entire picture with this, and sprinkle white powdered laundry soap on your picture. You will have a textured snowscape when it dries!

Sandpainting

Sandpainting grew up among the Indian tribes of the dessert Southwest United States. The Indian artist poured powdered rock or sand of different colors on a flatbed of sand. This technique demands considerable skill. The Indians made them impermanent so they had to be made new for each occasion. They had traditional designs that were used. See the Indian signs and symbols at the end of this lesson. The main use of sand painting was for "healing." Sandpainting of today is a work of art that can be purchased and enjoyed by everyone. It is done primarily by the Indians of Arizona and New Mexico. Designs are put on heavy masonite or tile and the colored sand is glued to the board so that people can purchase a sandpainting and put it in their home to enjoy. Look at the simple Indian designs on the following page. Each sand painting has a center of interest. This is what you look at first in the design. Young children can learn the concept of texture by feeling the sandpainting. Working with sand is lots of fun. Let's do a sand painting.

Indians did artwork with very primitive materials. They used berries for paint. What might they have used for a paint brush? Younger children might enjoy going outside and getting a small tree branch and then hammering it into a brush. They might also enjoy using squashed berries as the paint and then doing the picture on tree bark. Well, let's get back to sandpainting. Have the younger children make a very simple Indian design on a small piece of poster board. You will need to have available different colors of sand.

Sand can be purchased easily at a craft store. You can also add dry tempera paint to regular sand and shake this up in a jar to get a separate color of sand. Allow students to fill one area in at a time with white craft glue, and then sprinkle on colored sand. Now blow away the extra sand and repeat the process. Very young children can make a design on sandpaper and color it very heavily with crayons. This will look similar to a sandpainting. Older students need to focus on design. They need to make a balanced design with a center of interest. When they have this lightly penciled in, allow them to use colored sand in the same procedure as the younger children. If you just have one color of sand, you can allow them to cover a whole sheet of mat board with white sand. Allow this to dry and paint an Indian design on the composition. Offer older students the challenge of making an Indian design in pencil that has the look of a sandpainting. This should have the look of sand; this is called implied texture. It would be quite a time consuming and painstaking task similar to the technique used in pointillism. Look up pointillism in the encyclopedia. You can also do a picture on a piece of sandpaper with crayon and then turn it over on a piece of separate paper. Use an iron on medium temperature; it will look like pointillism.

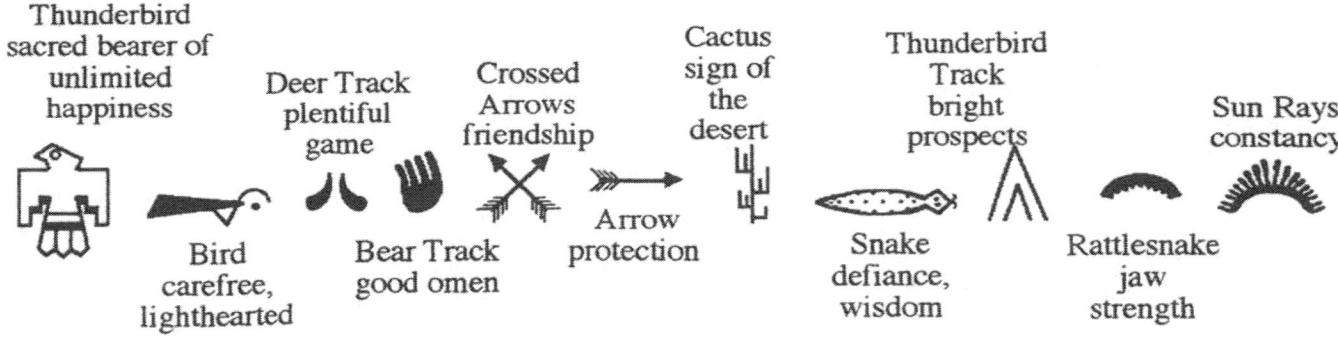

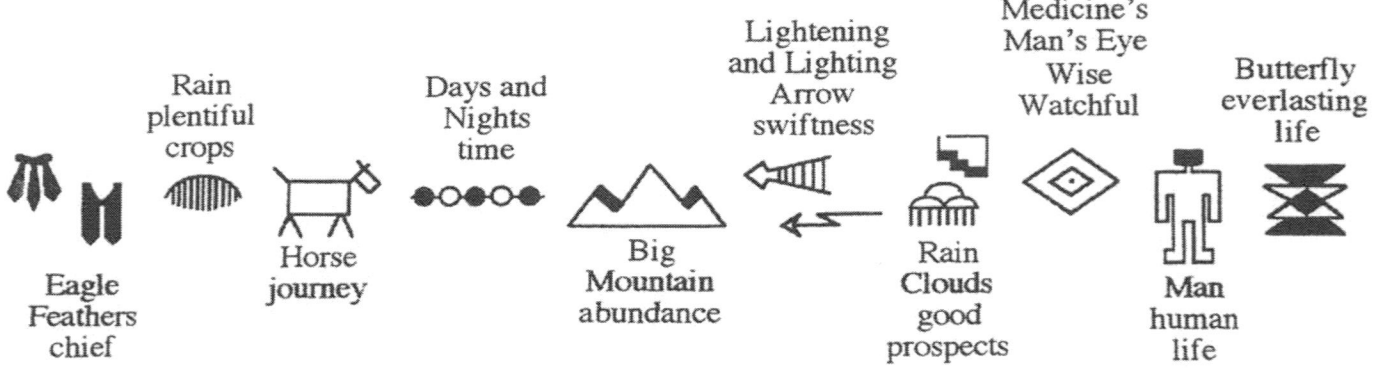

Robert Fulton --- Artist and Scientist

Robert Fulton was a very well known American artist who studied painting in England. He was also an inventor. Some people even called him the American Leonardo da Vinci because of his great inventions and his artwork. In 1807, Robert Fulton's first steamboat, the Clermont, sailed up the Hudson River from New York to Albany. It went 150 miles in only 32 hours. From 1820 to 1860 riverboats on the Mississippi went from only 60 to nearly 1000 in numbers. Look at the picture of this Fulton Steamboat. Use the directions to draw a similar steamboat. Color your boat with crayons or oil pastels and do your water and sky with blue watercolor.

Sheep Versus Cattle

During the nineteenth century, the cattlemen of the west considered the sheepherders to be their enemy. They resented the intrusion of the sheep on the open plain that they considered to be only for cattle. They felt that the sheep ate the grass too close to the roots. They said the grass was further damaged by the sharp hooves of the sheep. This picture is from *Frank Leslie's Illustrated Newspaper*, October 28, 1882.

Here is a wonderful project to do. Get a white piece of construction paper and write on it with a blue, black, gray, etc. magic marker. Make sure it is not a permanent marker. Remember how the colors ran when you got a paper wet when you were walking home in the rain? Let your paper get sprinkled on purpose and use the runny blots to make a design in the sky. Use colors that would be similar to a stormy sky. Let the paper dry and then put your sheep herd on the bottom. Use a sponge to make the sheep look like sheep. See directions. Take a second piece of paper. Talk about a realistic design and an abstract design. Now make one paper into an abstract design. This will be a design that is nonobjective. You don't know what it is, it is like nothing from real life, but it is an interesting design. Make your second picture have lots of action and movement, but be a realistic design of a sheep stampede. Which type of art do you prefer?

Sheep

Drawing a sheep is very simple. Because of the unique texture of wool, an interesting way to make a sheep is to do a sponge painting. Painting with sponges and watercolor, acrylic paint or ink gives the sheep an appearance of wool. A sponge painting is one technique you can use to imitate a style of painting called Impressionism. Impressionism is like a quick glance at something. There is a lack of detail. Do the outline of the sheep first, and then using a sponge start with the dark areas and work toward the light. Make sure you don't have too much water on your sponge! You may want to test your color, texture or dampness on another piece of paper before you start working on your pencil drawing. When making a herd of sheep, be sure sheep in the foreground are larger than sheep in the background.

The Cattle Drive

The cattle drive was an important occurrence in the west. This exciting picture was done by an artist in *Harper's Weekly*, October 19, 1867. It was the first picture of a cattle drive to appear in the nation's illustrated press. Notice the movement in the sky of the picture. First, get some watercolors and heavy paper or water color paper. Now wet the top half and drop storm colors in large drops on the paper (dark blue, gray, black yellow). Take a blow hair dryer or a straw and blow the colors to make them look like a stormy sky. Let the paper dry and then try to duplicate this picture. Make sure the cattle in the foreground are larger, and the background are smaller.

Pioneer Dolls

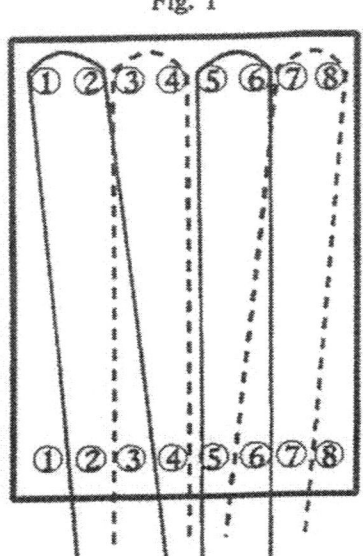
Fig. 1

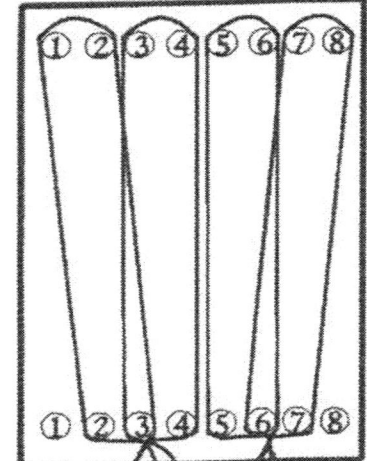
Fig. 2

These wonderful woven dolls are popular in the Ozark hills. There is a lady close to us who sells these character dolls and tells the story of pioneers making these dolls and then hanging them on the chinking of the log cabins. You can make character dolls of important people in American history. Follow the directions and make your own pioneer doll.

1. Nails are 1/2 inch to 1/4 inch apart on frame.
2. Always use flat head nails to keep the fabric from slipping.
3. Make 4 separate long strips for warp of loom, the vertical strips. Always clip end at an angle to reduce lumps.
4. Loop vertical strips over nails as shown on diagram, (Fig.1) stringing them in the correct order.
5. Always tie in a square knot as tight as possible against the nails (Fig.?). If the strings are not taut, you cannot weave.
6. Weaving fabric can be any width up to 2 inches wide.
7. Leave tail on warp threads at least 2 inches long. This will become the foot.
8. When weaving, use the warp threads between 2 and 3, and 6 and 7 as one warp thread since these threads are overlapped. Separate only when nearing the top for the arms.
9, First you make the feet, tuck under the four warp threads with best looking thread on top. Take enough yarn and wrap all four layers and tie into a foot shape using the loose ends as the core of the foot.
10. To start weaving, tie on your horizontal weaving thread, or woof thread, make one simple knot around threads at #6. This will be considered your over weave. When you run out of fabric, simply tuck angled end thru to back in the row below. There is no need to tie off.
11. If you are weaving a man, weave three outer strings on either side (nails 1, 2, 3, and 6,7, 8) into the legs. Weave each leg separately and when you get to the crotch area, tie the two center threads, and then weave all the threads together until you get to the waist area. Now change colors for the shirt.

Weave a woman all the way across on the loom (long skirt).

12. To form arms use only the outside two warp strings (nails 1 and 2 and 7 and 8).
When complete, clip only the arms off of the loom. Clip warp thread between these nails and tie knot to hold weaving.
13. Bend arms backwards and tie tails of hands to fabric at the hip line.
14. To weave face, use about 2 yards of skin colored yarn doubled. Tie on weave 5,
pulling very tautly to form neck, let loose gradually to form roundness for the face.
15. Weave face using vertical threads 3,4,5, and 6.
16. When face is complete to the ear line, start tying the hair on using three pieces of
yarn, each 3" long, each time you reach warps 3 and 6.

17. Use comb and comb hair yarn to look fuzzy.
18. Glue the back of the hair onto the head. This makes the face more permanent. Shape the hair around the back of the head and glue to appear like hair. Cut head warp threads off of the frame.
19. To form eyes and nose cut several 2" pieces of appropriate colored yarn and knot in the middle.
20. Place nose and eye knots on face and poke yarn to backside of face vertically. Add other details as you finish your doll. You will find innovative, creative ways to dress your doll up to look like the character it is supposed to be.

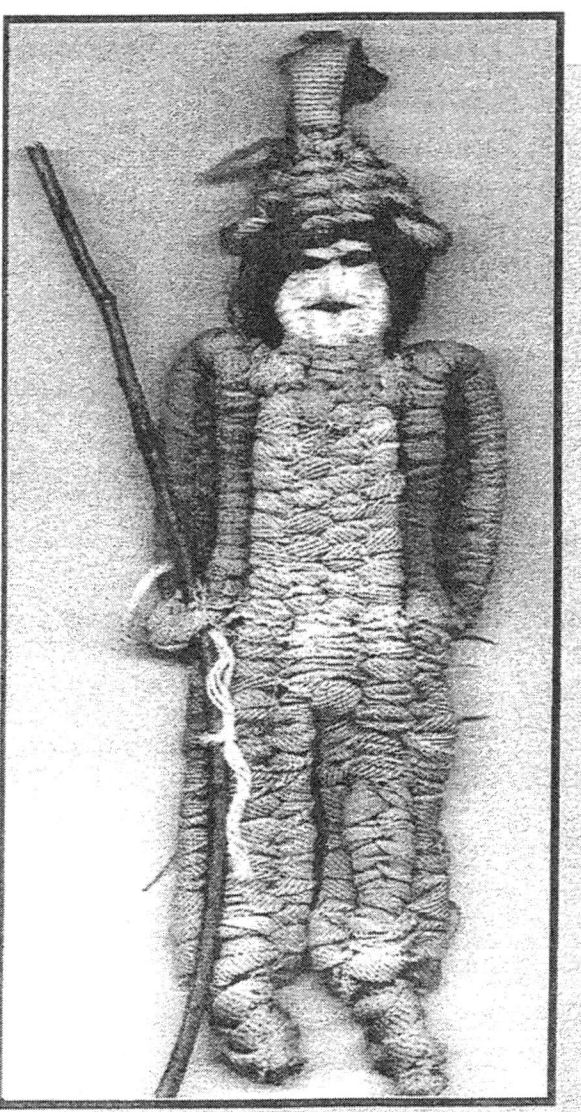

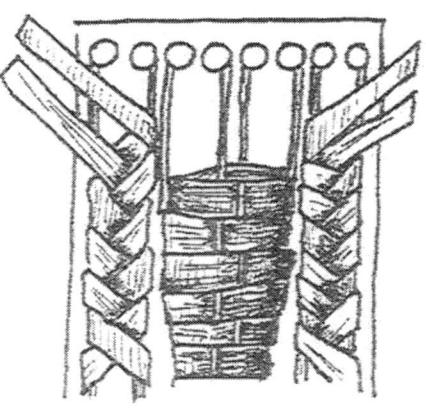

Rebus

A rebus was something that was used in the classroom of early America. A symbol is something that represents something else. A rebus is a representation of various words using symbols, pictures,

letters and numbers which represents a certain word or group of words. In early America, rebus puzzles were used in the classroom to teach independent thinking, logic and reason. Today a rebus can be used to teach English or help people learn to read and write. Early civilizations used pictures to tell a story or communicate something on stone or cave walls. In archaeology, a petroglyph is a carving or line drawing on rock, especially one made by prehistoric people. Early man made pictures to serve as records for hunting, tribal life and war. Pictures could also be sent as messages. A sun might mean one day. Two special marks beside the sun might mean two days. These signs are called pictographs.
On the following page is a picture of a petroglyph. Many Indians used pictures to communicate. They told the story on hides of animals as well as on rock. See the Indian signs and symbols on the lesson Sandpainting.

Write a paragraph about something special to you. Younger children can just make one sentence into a rebus. If they cannot as yet write, they can draw pictures. Now take each word separately and see what letter or symbol or picture you can think of to use in place of each word. Do you believe someone can easily translate your rebus?

Have students design a game show using the rebus for the game. Have them design at least ten rebus puzzles. Now allow two teams to see who solves the rebus puzzles first. Early man made pictures to serve as records for hunting, tribal life and war. Pictures could also be sent as messages. A sun might mean one day. Two special marks beside the sun might mean two days. These signs are called pictographs. Another good idea for this project is to take a brown paper bag and wad it into a ball. Unwad an wad the paper several times before flatting it out to paint on it. Use tea or brown water color paint and paint the paper. You will now have paper that looks like leather. Now use oil pastels and put an Indian design on the paper. Cut your paper in the shape of a hide. See Sandpainting lesson for Indian signs and symbols.

B = bee	8 = ate
D + R = deer	N + E + any
N + Q = thank-you	R = are
U = you	N + M = L = animal
3 = tree	

Pictographs

Early man made pictures to serve as records for hunting, tribal life and war. Pictures could also be sent as messages. A sun might mean one day. Two special marks beside the sun might mean two days. These signs are called pictographs.

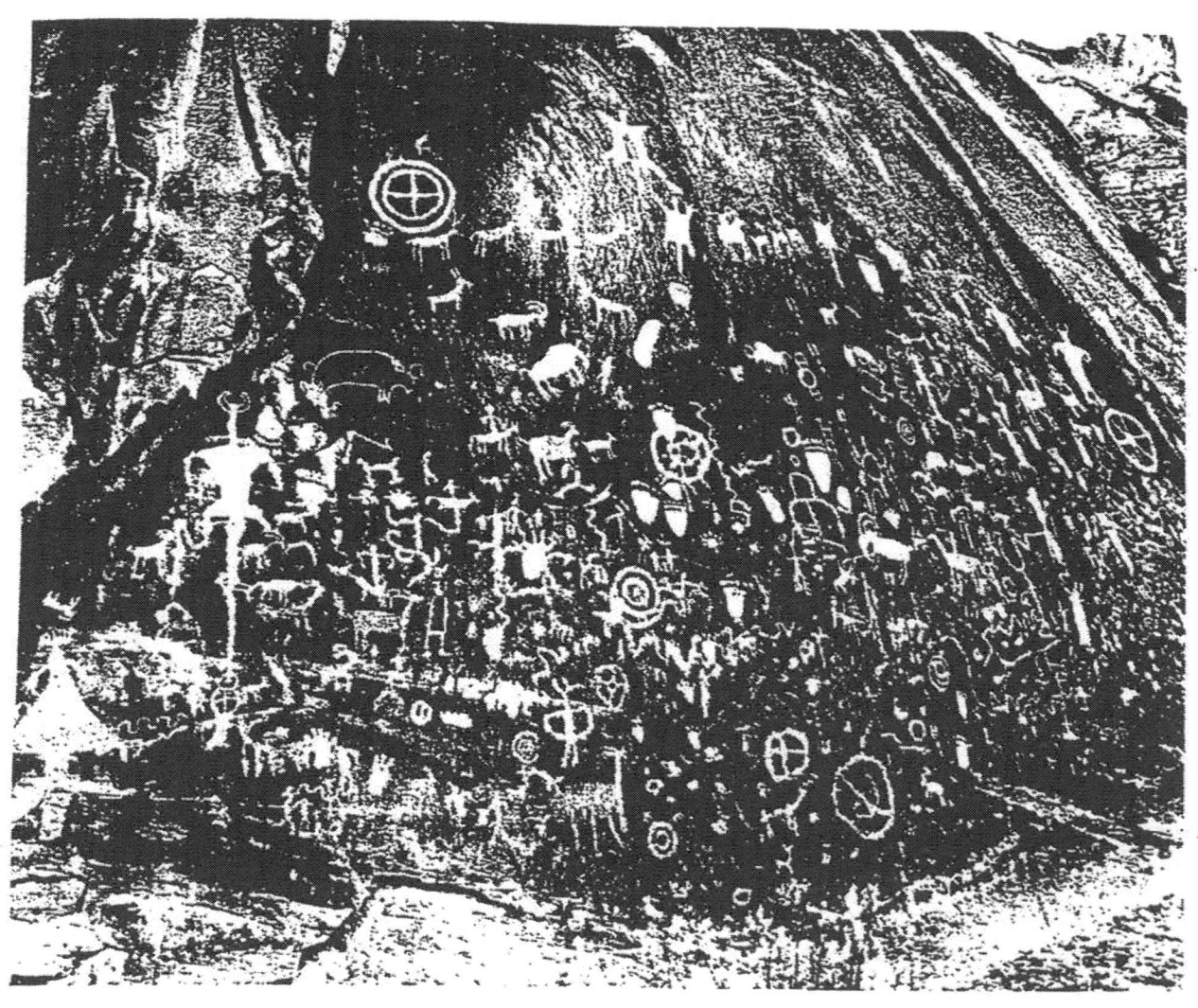

The Avalanche

Many perils occurred to the early pioneers and miners in the old west. The picture is of some prospectors in the mountains above Leadville taken by surprize by an avalanche. The picture was seen in *Harper's Weekly* on September 1, 1888.

Paper Quilling

Paper quilling is an art form that began during the Middle Ages. It was first practiced by nuns in the convents of Europe. The nuns would do very elaborate pictures out of paper. In early America, paper quilling was practiced by ladies as a very economical art form. You can even purchase antique paper quilling pictures from early America. Paper quilling is very simply taking long strips of paper and rolling them into small wheels. These little wheel shapes are then used to make designs and pictures. Art that you can go all the way around is called

Cut paper into strips 1/4 to 1/2 inch.
Roll the strips into little circles.
Pinch to change circle
into other shapes

three-dimensional. Art that has a raised surface is two-dimensional. Look at the shapes made by paper quilling on this page. Paper quilling that is not three-dimensional is two-dimensional. The quilled shapes are glued to a flat surface. Mat board would work the best. When you paper quill, roll your shapes on to a small metal rod or a pencil. There is a certain tool you can purchase to do paper quilling. You can glue your shapes together with white craft glue, or you can use a glue gun.

Look at the free hanging shapes on this page. Have younger students make five different shapes, and attach them with string to a stick or the mobile base shown.

Allow older children to make an elaborate paper quilling design. Perhaps they want to make an ornate letter by adding quilling around it. They might want to do a flower design. When they are done, it might look beautiful to spray the completed design with gold or silver spray paint.

The End of the Civil War

Ulysses S. Grant

Robert E. Lee

One of the saddest parts of American history is the Civil War. The north and the south fought over the states rights and slavery issue. Many men died on both sides. Sometimes brother would fight brother. Look at this copyright free picture done by an artist at the time of the signing of the peace treaty. General Grant, the great northern general, sat down with General Lee, the great southern general, and they signed a treaty. Other great military men watched. Look up General Stonewall Jackson and draw a battle scene that he was part of. Look up General Sherman and draw a battle scene he might have been part of. Notice how the men in the background look smaller than the men in the foreground. Now look at the lesson on one point perspective on the following page. Draw this great treaty scene, being sure to keep the room in perspective.

The surrender of Lee to Grant at the Appomattox Court House

One-Point Perspective

When you look down a rail road track or a highway, you can easily see a one point perspective. You can also see this effect inside a large room. A good way to learn one-point perspective is to draw the inside of a room. This is better than just doing a railroad track, because you are doing four planes in three dimensional space instead of only.

In a one - point perspective, all lines that are vertical will always be vertical and remain parallel to all other vertical lines. All horizontal lines in a one - point perspective will be horizontal unless they are aligned with the VP.

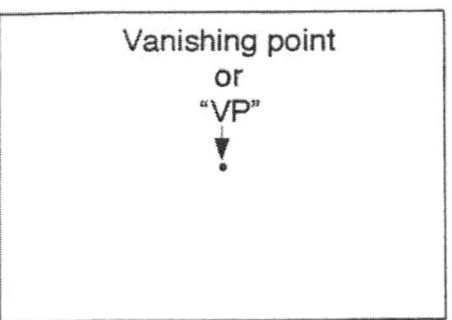

Vanishing point or "VP"

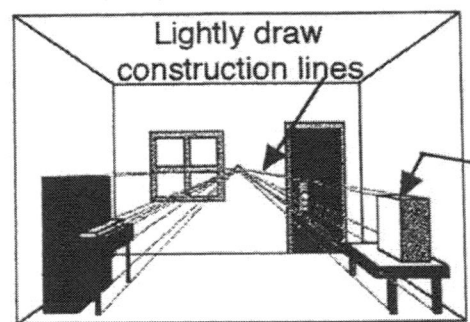

Lightly draw construction lines

Lines drawn from the corners of your objects to the VP.

"X" is created by drawing a line from the VP to the corners of the page.

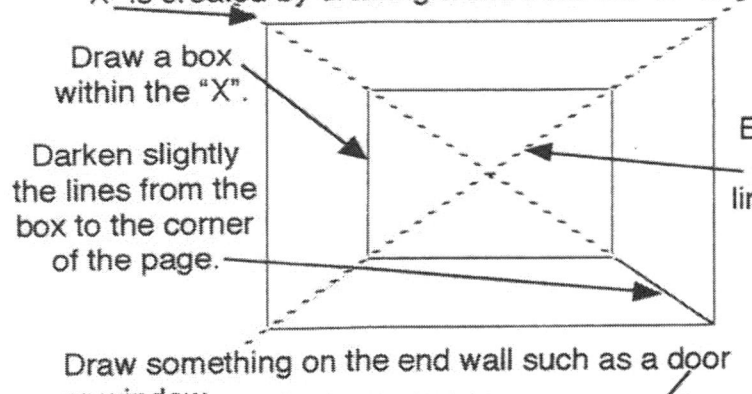

Draw a box within the "X".

Darken slightly the lines from the box to the corner of the page.

Erase the lines in the box.

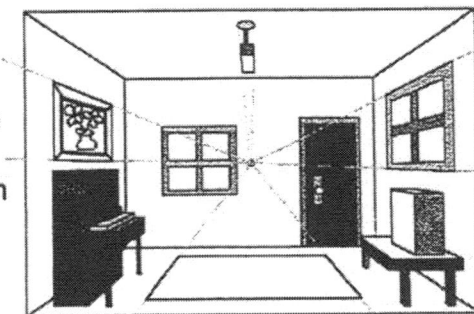

Keep your lines light so they can be easily erased.

Draw something on the end wall such as a door or window.

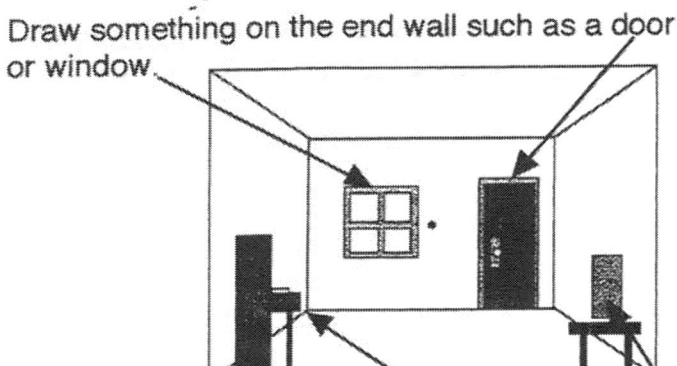

FINISHED ONE- POINT PERSPECTIVE

Draw furniture in your room by first drawing the near end in profile.

This is a piano and a T.V.

The Civil War

In the same way that the great artist Benjamin West was assigned to be the historical artist for the court of King George, Edwin Forbes was assigned to cover the Army of the Potomac during the Civil War for the publication Frank Leslie's Illustrated Newspaper. He dutifully followed this army from 1862 to the siege of Petersburg in 1864. In the picture below was where most of the army spent the winter of 1862. Stew and biscuits were probably the main staple of food. Do you notice that the third man in this picture was meant to look like Walt Whitman, a company man known well by the artist? A wagon train is shown coming down the hill. It was very difficult feeding the huge number of troops. Forbes obviously drew this landscape with great care. Notice how the things in the foreground of the picture are larger and the things in the background much smaller. Notice the trees on the horizon line. Notice the flag. Can you copy this picture with great care? Try to copy just one small area of it and make it very large.

Newspapers in the Camp

Even soldiers were very hungry for news. It seems as though the troops were either in a rush to battle or in a waiting mode. In this scene the union troops are reading the newspapers. There are homemade stools making one think the troops were in a waiting period. The pup tents of World Wars I and II were similar to these tents. Can you make a picture of the perfect war camp? What would be comfortable and what would not?

Marching in the Rain

Look at the picture below. Do you not get the feel of hopelessness by just looking at this picture? Diagonal lines show movement in art. The rain in the sky is shown by using diagonal lines. The paper said "The column presented a soaked and bedraggled appearance." Is that the feeling you get from this picture? Do a picture of soldiers in the rain. You can easily make a picture look wet by using water color paints, but try to do your whole picture in black lines with pen and ink.

Praising the Lord

This scene is definitely one of joy and happiness. Forbes said, "The old mother dropped on her knees and said "Bless de Lord" and the father uncovered his head." As the war was ending, many scenes of emotion were probably captured by various artists. Can you do a scene with a cross on the hillside, or some other scene that is full of emotion? What kind of movements will the people be making?

The Beginning of the Cities -- Industry in America

At the very end of the eighteenth century, machinery and factories were unheard of. But England was ordering and making things in factories to make production much better and things were to change in America. England introduced machinery, and in America a big reward was offered to anyone who could build a cotton spinning machine. Three men were very important in bringing industry to America. Samuel Slater memorized the way the cotton spinning machines were built, and brought them to American in 1790. Eli Whitney was a teacher and invented a simple machine that removed seeds from the cotton called the cotton gin. Another American that was a catalyst in the Industrial Revolution was Francis Lowell who visited England in 1810 and was able to visit a cloth making factory and memorize and understood how it worked. He came back and developed factories in the Industrial North. America would have many cityscapes thanks to these three great Americans.

Making a cityscape is an exciting project for young people. You might go over several famous cities before you begin. The skyline of the city of New York or Chicago are well known to many people. When children begin, assign the younger children to cut and paste a cityscape. They can either use wall paper patterns cut in rectangles or they can use magazine pictures. Allow them to color water at the bottom of the cityscape and then glue and paste their different rectangles vertically on the paper. You can talk about vertical lines and also patterns. You can talk about

reflection and try to get the children to duplicate in the water what they have cut and pasted on their picture. Older students can make a sunset sky. I suggest using colored chalks, remembering to color very opaquely, not letting white show through. Now allow them to use black charcoal or marker and duplicate a city skyline. I once had a student that did such a beautiful job at this that he sold the finished work to a travel agency.

Thomas Nast--Editorial Cartoonist

September 27, 1840 was the birthday of Thomas Nast. There are many pictures we use today that we owe to the famous cartoonist Thomas Nast. He was America's first well known *editorial cartoonist*.. Because of his work, we have the political symbol of the Republican party, Uncle Sam, and the well loved caricature of Santa Claus to name just a few. A person who does editorial cartoons communicates visually. It is a powerful medium to sway opinion. Look at the famous political cartoon about the Republican and Democratic Party. What do you think Thomas Nast is saying about the them in the cartoon? He was most instrumental about seeing that the infamous "Boss Tweed" come to justice by using his outrageous cartoons. In September and October, we will hear about upcoming elections. Go to a large metropolitan paper and look at the editorial cartoons. Do you feel that the artists communicated visually what they wanted to say? Now come up with an idea for an editorial cartoon. It can be about any topic, as long as you communicate your opinion visually. Maybe they are eliminating access to your favorite swimming place in the creek.....maybe you believe your town needs to be involved more in taking care of the homeless....you might want to communicate your position on a political issue...

A cariacture is a picture where you exaggerate a person's features. It has been called visual satire. Look this up in your dictionary. Now do a caricature of a friend of yours. Be sure and have some fun and exaggerate their features.

First Assignment at age 15 (never published)

First political cartoon

The symbol of the Democratic Party

Symbol of the Republican Party

Santa as we know him.

George Washington Carver

George Washington Carver was one of the truly great Americans. He is a role model in all ways to all Americans everywhere. Not only was he a scientific and artistic genius, he was a role model in character as well. He started his professional life as an artist, drawing the beautiful plants and flowers that he loved so much. He overcame the very difficult circumstance of slavery, got admitted to college against great odds, and became a great leader. He even overcame the handicaps of ill health and stuttering. He had a deep belief and faith in God that showed in his attitudes about his discoveries. He never patented a single invention, "God gave them to me," he said, "How can I sell them to someone else?"

Although he could number the presidents among his friends, he always took time for the common man. Choose a certain flower (plant) you would like to study. Do a picture of this flower, making it as beautiful as possible. Because you like this flower, you want other people to appreciate it and notice it for its great beauty. Now do a scientific drawing of the flower. Label all of the parts. Scientists and artists are both observers of nature.

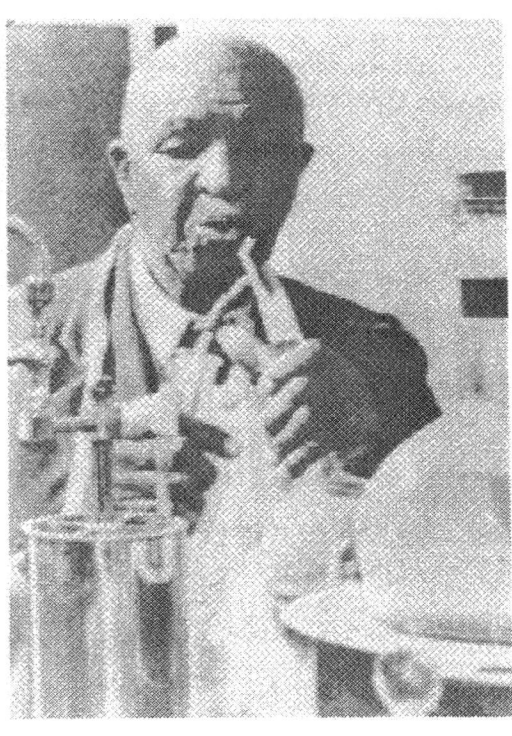

Which picture of the flower do you like the best?

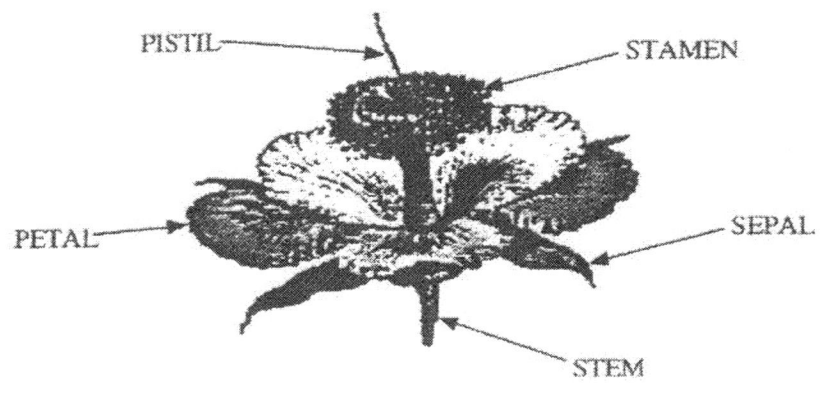

The Teddy Bear

Clifford Berryman was an editorial cartoonist that had a profound influence on American culture.

What would a study of American history be without mention of the Teddy Bear? How did it all start? An artist was the catalyst for the famous toy that has given comfort to thousands of children worldwide. In the year 1902, our President Teddy Roosevelt went hunting in the southern United States. His companions caught a poor little bear who looked as if he had been burned by a forest fire. They tied him to a tree and told the president to shoot him. He refused. Berryman did a cartoon about this event. A man named Morris Michtom, a toy maker, was inspired to make two toy bears. He wrote to the president and asked if he could use his name for the new toys. Roosevelt replied, " I don't think my name is likely to be worth much in the toy bear business, but you are welcome to use it." The rest is history.

Let's make some bears. Younger children can follow directions for making bears. Older children can try to draw a realistic bear-- making the fur look like real fur.

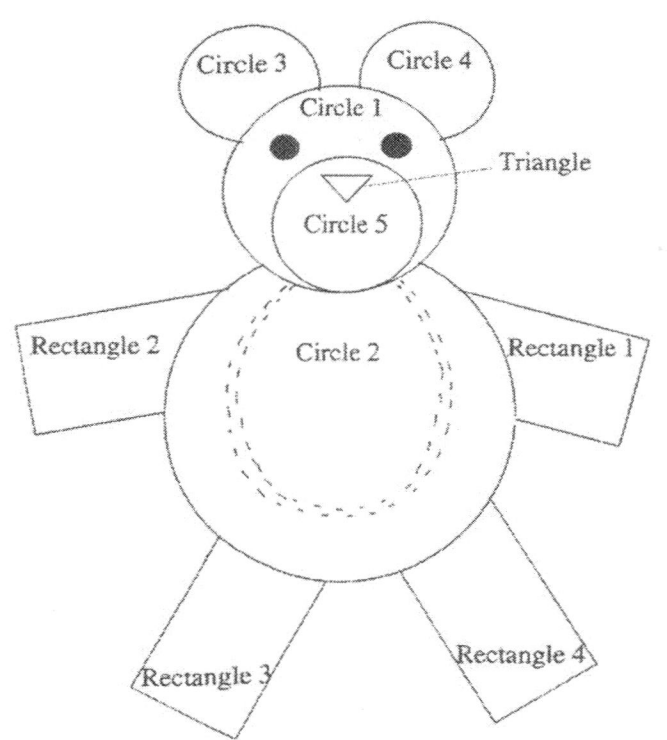

Purple Mountain's Majesty

Have you ever heard of a paper and fabric collage? Have children find a beautiful landscape picture of a landmark or landscape in America. This is a picture of the Yosemite Valley in California. It can be poster size; the larger the better! They can either draw this lightly in pencil, or use the actual picture for their collage. If children choose to glue materials on the actual picture, use white craft glue to glue it to a piece of poster board or mat board. If they choose to draw this landscape, draw this on the poster board. Now obtain some wallpaper books (free), various used magazines, buttons, fabric scraps, cotton, etc. Cut and paste these materials to the landscape. Use your imagination and add patterns, animals and textures to your finished picture. Talk about vertical, horizontal and diagonal lines with the children. Talk about various patterns. Sometimes you can go into a children's bookstore and ask for throw away book covers to use as a background. Now talk about this famous place and what it means in our history.

Old Fashioned Christmas

Here are some ornaments that would work well in an "Old Fashioned Christmas." In the early days of our country, ornaments were made from paper, popcorn, cranberries, fans, cards, oranges, etc. Here are some ideas. If possible, go on a family expedition and find your special tree. If you live in the city, even going to the tree lot can be lots of fun. It is so special to smell the fresh smell of pine or spruce, and know that is your own special tree. You can even buy a tree in a pot and then plant it later in memory of your special Christmas. One ornament to make is done with paper chains. Use old music books or magazines. Chances are most people in early America couldn't afford to buy special paper. Use flour and water to make a paste to glue your chains together. You can also make a nice ornament by taking old Christmas cards and cutting out the faces. Make a shape of a Victorian couple(see sample), and glue face on and then glue(can use regular cotton balls) cotton--use paste--on the cardboard backing. Hole punch the top and tie a ribbon in it so you can hang on tree. These are very Victorian ornaments. Orange baskets would sometimes be high on the limbs of the "Old Fashioned Tree." Take an orange and cut it in half. Attempt to keep the orange in good condition as you take the center out. You will have a

basket shape. Let this dry out and glue a ribbon handle on the basket and fill it with goodies. Use old music books and cut shapes and hang them on tree. You can also use old music paper and roll scrolls and glue them together and tie with a ribbon. The ideas are endless. Make a list of things you might have available in 1880 to decorate your tree. Now design an ornament from these.

Currier and Ives

Currier and Ives is the name of a firm of well known lithographers who captured American life in the 1800's in pictures. They showed Americans at work and play. They did pictures of American ships, sports of the times, the American gold rush, and many historic events of the day. Currier and Ives worked separately until 1857, when all of their prints carried the joint name. A good project for children to do to remember these famous artists is a foam meat tray print. Save your meat trays---especially the large ones and cut the frame off of the tray. Make sure this is well cleaned. Now allow children to draw a scene on the tray with pencil. A winter snow scene is a good idea. We still purchase Christmas cards today with scenes from Currier and Ives. When the scene is drawn and indented, have children paint with tempera paint in a dark blue to begin. Now allow them to print the scene on the paper. Each successive print will be lighter. Which do they prefer? Allow them to use other colors after washing the tray.

Mount Rushmore

Mount Rushmore is a solid granite cliff 25 miles west of Rapid City, South Dakota. Carved into this cliff are the faces of 4 U.S. Presidents: George Washington, Thomas Jefferson, Abraham Lincoln, and Theodore Roosevelt. George Washington's head is about 60 feet tall. If Washington had the rest of his body carved under his head he would be over 465 feet tall. A man named Gutzon Borglum began this memorial in 1927 and worked on it for 14 years until he died in 1941. His son named Lincoln completed his work. Gutzon Borglum first made a scale model of his project. His model was scaled so that one inch equaled one foot. It was then lifted to the top of the cliff so that the workman could use it to guide their work. The men supervised by Borglum and guided by the model used drills and dynamite to complete the monumental task. Have students design a Mt. Rushmore of today. Allow them to choose four famous Americans and mold their faces together. After they have finished their design, allow them to take a bar of soap and try to sculpt a face. Rock carving is subtractive sculpture. That means that once something comes off, you cannot glue it back on. It is very different from clay or wax sculpture. It is amazing that this work of art looks so real when the medium used was so technically difficult.

Can you see Mount Rushmore looking like one of these groupings? Who would you choose to complete your carving of a great work of art? Everyone will have a variety of ideas. You might choose a grouping of great people in the Bible. You might choose a grouping of famous women of character, or famous musicians. Draw your grouping in pencil first, and if you are up to a challenge, purchase modeling clay, sculpy, or real pottery clay and make your sculpture.

Calendars

Creating calendars can be an imaginative and creative activity for children of all ages. I collect calendars and never stop being amazed at the wonderful variety. A field trip to your local gift store might be in order. In the same way that an artist creates a card, an artist creates a calendar. Calendar ideas and card ideas are often sought after by large companies like Hallmark. A freelance artist will send in some ideas and the company will decide if they will pay the artist for their work and purchase the rights to publish it. Any good idea has a center of interest; a dominant point that draws the observer into the picture. A theme for a calendar would need to be carried out throughout the calendar. Make an American History Calendar. You can create a blank calendar on the computer, or send to Visual Manna and order blank calendars on heavy stock paper. Now allow students to create their own calendar with their greatest area of interest in American history as the theme. Talk about the idea of copyrighting their idea and perhaps marketing it as an educational calendar. A border is something that goes all the way around a picture. A border can be very elaborate or very plain. Would they like to put a border around each picture? For an important web site with pictures of early America go to:

http://earlyamerica.com/portraits/index.html

SIGNING THE DECLARATION OF INDEPENDENCE

Tiffany Glass

When you are speaking about American works of accomplishment in the arts, you cannot neglect the great accomplishment of Tiffany Glass. We were recently in the Indianapolis Art Museum and were able to see a beautiful stained glass window made by Tiffany Glass. The Tiffany family is also well known for jewelry designing. The name Charles Tiffany stands today for the highest quality in jewelry. Louis Tiffany is the family member who is known for developing

Tiffany Favrile glass. In 1875, he used colored glass to make vases, tiles, and other objects that were very beautiful and high quality. In 1919, he started a foundation for American artists. There are many exciting projects to do that are associated with stained glass. One of my favorites is to make a stained glass window design and then color this very dark with oil pastels. By dark, this means to make sure the design is opaque ----- you cannot see any white through the colors. Now brush cooking oil over the entire design. The colors will have a wonderful transparent quality. Another good idea is to use water color paint for your stained glass design. Now fill a glue bottle up with half part white craft glue and half black tempera paint. Use the mixture to divide the colors of your stained glass window. When doing a project relating to jewelry, our favorite is to use modeling clay (you can obtain this at a local discount store) and allow students to design a medallion. They can then build a wall around their design so plaster of paris can be poured in. Mix the plaster, pour

in the mold and allow to set (approximately ten minutes). Remove the clay and you have a wonderful piece of jewelry that can be painted to suit the creator. Remember that your mold will have to be made in reverse. Everything that sticks out will stick in after it is poured and every thing looking left will be right. Sometimes I am amazed at what comes out of the mold. Almost never is it exactly what I had envisioned! For a great web site on this topic go to: http://arts-crafts.com/archive/tiffany.html

Pottery

Pottery includes all kinds of dishes, tiles, and other items that are made from baked clay. From the rich pottery produced by the American Indians to the fine brands of pottery that is distinctly American such as Rockwood or Marblehead Pottery; America has produced a rich heritage in this art. Rockwood Pottery was a high quality artistic pottery that used an air brush to make a soft edged design. American Pottery also includes old Pennsylvania - German tulip ware. This was called tulip ware because often tulips were seen in the pottery. This was seen in the 1800's and is even reviving today in popularity. Allow children to make some pots out of modeling clay or sculpy. Both can be purchased at your local discount store. To come up with an original design, artists first make the pot out of clay and then make a mold so the pot can be reproduced many times for sale to large numbers of people. Sometimes you can go to an art show or craft store and purchase hand made pots, but that is rare. Usually you go to a store and buy a pot that has been poured into a mold and mass produced. Have children make a pot with the idea that this pot will be made into a mold and sold to thousands of people. Below are two methods to build pots.

COIL BUILDING

Score both pieces of clay and put together with slip.

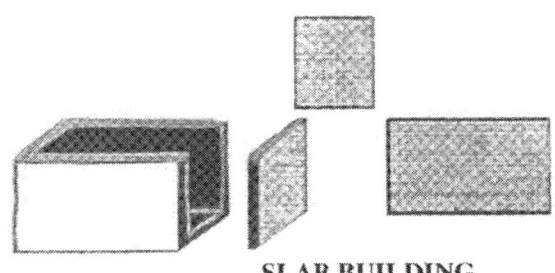

SLAB BUILDING

American Indians ---
The Original Americans

This is a pictorial tribute to the American Indian. Southwestern art is very popular today. I was privileged, while teaching in Oklahoma, to get to know the Indian artist Troy Anderson. He does marvelous paintings with an Indian theme. His pictures about the "Trail of Tears" are very moving. When I taught Indian arts and crafts at a school in Watts, Oklahoma, he would come in and encourage the young Indian students. His struggle for recognition as an artist included over five years of working at a canning company during the day and painting at night. After much effort, he now supports his family with his marvelous works of art. There are many works of art that are part of Indian culture. Some Indians make elaborate God's Eyes. Bead work is also a traditionally Indian craft. To make an interesting picture that looks like a bead design, you can use coarse sandpaper and crayons. Color a design on a strip of sandpaper and then iron the back of the sandpaper on a piece of colored paper. It will look like a beaded design. Look at these pictures of Indians. Now draw your own Indian on brown butcher paper or a brown paper bag using black and white charcoal. Dramatic results can be achieved. Cutting the paper in the shape of an animal hide will enhance the design.

NEW YORK CITY--THE CENTER OF ART ?

Did you know that there was once a time when America was the center of the art world? Yes, after World War II, Jackson Pollack began the great movement that was abstract art. He painted by dribbling and dripping on gigantic canvases. This was very novel and a revelation in the art world. Some people still today do not appreciate abstract art. It is a matter of opinion. What do you think? We have another modern pioneer in the art world from New York and that is Andy Warhol. He did gigantic Campbell Soup Cans and famous people such as the Mona Lisa and Marilyn Monroe. He developed the use of the silk screen. The jury may still be out on this to many people, however, when speaking of American art, it is difficult not to mention

these two giants of the world of modern art. There are other American artists of note in this movement, however, these two were true pioneers. These pictures are similar to the works of Warhol and Pollack created by Richard Jeffus.

The Merging of Science and Art in America's History

We all know of the fascinating combination of science and art in the inventions and anatomical and biological drawings of the Renaissance master Leonardo da Vinci, but there are few people who know of the great American inventors who were also artists. Samuel Morse was known as an extremely gifted painter, until at the age of 42, he decided to complete an idea that he had for an invention later called a telegraph. The rest is history. His heart was in doing historical paintings the most famous of which is "The Old House of Representatives." In the times that he lived, an artist had to paint portraits to make a living and he dutifully did so for a time. Robert Fulton, the inventor of the steamboat is sometimes called the Leonardo da Vinci of America, being a master artist, yet only known for his invention. George Washington Carver, the great scientist was also an artist and even exhibited his work in Chicago. He did wonderful pictures of the plants and flowers he so loved. Following are two more great American artists who are also scientists, with project suggestions. Here is a copy of a picture by C. W. Peale called "Exhuming the First American Mastodon." C. W. Peale was one of the most famous of the early American artists and even founded natural history and the first natural history museum. "He conceived of stuffing animals for his museum and placing each one in a still life setting backed by a picture of its natural environment." is a direct quote from Three Hundred Years of American Painting by Alexander Eliot. In 1801 he paid a farmer $300.00, a rifle, and some dresses, for permission to dig on his land and a large pile of bones. Although he was an artist, he was also quite a scientist. He was apprenticed at a young age to a saddle maker and then traded a

saddle for lessons in portraiture. He did so well a group of businessmen sent him to England to study with the great Benjamin West. (Although West is listed as an American artist, I believe he was more of a bridge to Europe as he spent most of his career there and was even appointed the historical artist to the court of King George.)
Peale went into the military in 1776 as a first lieutenant and spent time painting miniatures on Ivory for soldiers to sent home. Here is an exciting project. Allow students to make a miniature portrait on a round piece of poster board about 3"by 3." They can also do a detailed miniature painting of a landscape very dear to them. In Japan, when a plesiosaur was found on a fishing boat and photographed, the country honored the find by designing a postage stamp about the incident. Look at the picture of the mastodon dig and design a small postage stamp about this important event. Here is a make believe marble recipe. Make a small miniature circle by pouring this in a plastic lid--the smallest you can find. 1 cup of white glue, 1 cup water, Plaster of Paris, Tempera paint. Put some

water in a container and sprinkle with plaster until you get a creamy mixture---add your glue to the mixture along with some tempera paint that you streak to get a marble effect. Now pour into your mold. Paint your marble plaque. For a great web site go to http://sunsite.auc.dk/cgfa/cwpeale8.html on the net.

John James Audubon is one of the most famous of the American artists. He loved birds and was an avid hunter. According to <u>Three Hundred Years of American Painting</u> by Eliot, he wore the fringed buckskin of the frontiersman, with leggings, tomahawk and sheath knife. After a failing in business, at age 35, Audubon decided to paint hundreds of the birds he loved so much and reproduce them in a book. Audubon left his family and headed east to find a publisher for so vast a project. Finding little encouragement there, he headed to England. Eventually, he got 161 patrons from Britain, Europe and America to give $1000 each for his <u>Birds of America</u> and returned home in triumph. Sir Walter Besant said of him in 1837 "Brave is the exhibition of flowing locks; they flow over the ears and over the coat collars; you can smell the bear's grease across the street; and if these amaranthine locks were to be raised you would see the shiny coating of bear's grease upon the velvet collar below."

When Audubon first meant his wife, it is said he painted her picture. In water color first, and then salvaged the picture with an overlay of pastel. This mixture of mediums remained his main painting technique. Use the picture of how to draw a bird and make your drawing. Now do the picture in water color and then go over it with pastel. For

Audubon pictures go to http://www.carol.org/gemwww/sportingart/atun.html on the net.

It is my belief that art should be a catalyst for problem solving and original ideas. Both scientists and artists experiment to find out what happens when different elements are are mixed together. Imagination is required for both. When you draw something, you learn details and things about it that you might miss when just observing the object. Art is a lesson in discovery of nature. Surely these great scientists and inventors got their observation and problem solving skills to some degree by coming up with original ideas, problem solving, and inventing things in art.

Remington and the Setting Sun

Remington was a great western artist who captured the old west in America for us to enjoy visually. As the sun is truly setting on the "Old West" as we remember it from long ago, so things in our times are changing and dying out. If you were assigned to picture some aspect in our society today that is dying out because of modern technology and convenience, what would it be? Draw a picture of it.

Visual Manna
P.O. Box 553
Salem, MO 65560
573 - 729 - 2100
arthis@rollanet.org
visualmanna.nu

Petroglyphs
Discovery of America
Leif Erikson
1000 A.D.

Columbus discovers America 1492
Indian Pottery - Weaving

1620 Plymouth Colony
Great portrait artists - Copely, Peale, Stuart

Peale founded first Natural History Museum
1775 War for Independence

1776 Declaration of Independence
Trumball's Painting "Declaration of Independence."

George Washington First President
1789
"The Peaceable Kingdom"
Edward Hicks
Benjamin West

1812
War of 1812
"Old Ironsides"

1803 Louisiana purchase

Writers Longfellow, Emerson, Webster

1807
Robert Fulton, artist and inventor, produces the first successful steamboat

1822
Samuel Morse paints "The Old House of Representatives."

1826-1838 Audubon's "Birds of America," produced.

1836 Texas enters the Union
1837 - Telegraph Currier and Ives

1849 - California Gold Rush
George Caleb Bingham paints river pictures, Mark Twain - writer
Catlin, Remington, Russell picture the Old West

1860 - The Pony Express
Bierdstadt and Moran picture pristine American west
1865 - The Civil War
Forbes, Civil War artist, pictures the war

1876 - Telephone invented

1884 - Washington Monument completed

1890 - Mary Cassatt

Thomas Nast's Editorial Cartoons

1903 - Wright Brothers

1908 - Model T

1912 - Titanic sinks
1914 - 1918 World War I

1920 - First radio station
1922 - Lincoln Memorial completed
1924 - The Statue of Liberty donated -- sculptor - Bartholdi

Frank Lloyd Wright - America's greatest architect

1927 - Borglum began Mt. Rushmore
1929 - The Great Depression
1930 - The Locust Bowl
Georgia O'Keefe

1939-45 World War II
Artist - Norman Rockwell pictures America
Edward Hopper - Great American realist

1950's Abstract Movement
Jackson Pollock
Andy Warhol

66

MORE BOOKS FROM VISUAL MANNA

Art Through the Core series...
- Teaching American History Through Art
- Teaching Astronomy Through Art
- Teaching English Through Art
- Teaching History Through Art
- Teaching Literature Through Art
- Teaching Math Through Art
- Teaching Science Through Art
- Teaching Social Studies Through Art

Other Books...
- Art Adventures in Narnia
- Art Basics for Children
- Bible Arts & Crafts
- Christian Holiday Arts & Crafts
- Dragons, Dinosaurs, Castles and Knights
- Drawing, Painting and Sculpting Horses
- Expanding Your Horizons Through Words
- Indians In Art
- Master Drawing
- Preschool & Early Elementary Art Basics
- Preschool Bible Lessons
- Visual Manna 1: Complete Art Curriculum
- Visual Manna 2: Advanced Techniques

Books available at Rainbow Resource Center:
www.rainbowresource.com • 888.841.3456

Educating with art since 1992!

A Christian is one whose imagination should fly beyond the stars. Francis Schaeffer

His Lions

Contact *visualmanna@gmail.com* if you are interested in our Intern program. Students learn how to teach art, do murals for ministry, prepare an excellent portfolio, and much more. Go to **visualmanna.com** for information.

Free art lessons are available at **OurHomeschoolForum.com** and books are available at Rainbow Resource Center (**www.rainbowresource.com**). Try all our "Art Through the Core" series and other books as well! Make learning fun for kids!!! Sharon Jeffus teaches Art Intensives in person for the Landry Academy at **landryacademy.com**.

Made in the USA
Charleston, SC
30 August 2016